The Biography of Anne Frank

Stephanie Rogut

Annelies Marie (Anne) Frank was a German-born diarist. One of the most discussed Jewish victims of the Holocaust, she gained fame posthumously following the publication of The Diary of a Young Girl (originally Het Achterhuis; English: The Secret Annex), in which she documents her life in hiding from 1942 to 1944, during the German occupation of the Netherlands in World War II. It is one of the world's most widely known books and has been the basis for several plays and films.

Born in Frankfurt, Germany, she lived most of her life in or near Amsterdam, Netherlands, having moved there with her family at the age of four-and-a-half when the Nazis gained control over Germany. Born a German national, Frank lost her citizenship in 1941 and thus became stateless. By May 1940, the Franks were trapped in Amsterdam by the German occupation of the Netherlands. As persecutions of the Jewish population increased in July 1942, the family went into hiding in some concealed rooms behind a bookcase in the building where Anne's father worked. From then until the family's arrest by the Gestapo in August 1944, Anne kept a diary she had received as a birthday present, and wrote in it regularly. Following their arrest, the Franks were transported to concentration camps. In October or November 1944, Anne and her sister, Margot, were transferred to Bergen-Belsen concentration camp from Auschwitz, where they died (probably of typhus) a few months later. They were originally estimated by the Red Cross to have died in March, with Dutch authorities setting 31 March as their official date of death, but research by the Anne Frank House in 2015 suggests they more likely died in February.

Frank's father, Otto, the only survivor of the family, returned to Amsterdam after the war to find that her diary had been saved by one of the helpers, Miep Gies, and his efforts led to its publication in 1947. It was translated from its original Dutch version and first published in English in 1952 as The Diary of a Young Girl, and has since been translated into over 60 languages.

Early Life

Frank was born Annelies or Anneliese Marie Frank on 12 June 1929 at the Maingau Red Cross Clinic in Frankfurt, Germany, to Edith (née Holländer) and Otto Heinrich Frank. She had an older sister, Margot. The Franks were liberal Jews, and did not observe all of the customs and traditions of Judaism. They lived in an assimilated community of Jewish and non-

Jewish citizens of various religions. Edith was the more devout parent, while Otto was interested in scholarly pursuits and had an extensive library; both parents encouraged the children to read. At the time of Anne's birth the family lived in a house at Marbachweg 307, where they rented two floors. In 1931 the family moved to Ganghoferstrasse 24 in a fashionable liberal area called the Dichterviertel (Poets' Quarter). Both houses still exist.

In 1933, after Adolf Hitler's Nazi Party won the federal election, Edith Frank and the children went to stay with Edith's mother, Rosa, in Aachen. Otto Frank remained in Frankfurt, but after receiving an offer to start a company in Amsterdam, he moved there to organize the business and to arrange accommodations for his family. He began working at the Opekta Works, a company that sold fruit extract pectin, and found an apartment on the Merwedeplein

(Merwede Square) in the Rivierenbuurt neighbourhood of Amsterdam. By February 1934, Edith and the children had joined him in Amsterdam. The Franks were among 300,000 Jews who fled Germany between 1933 and 1939.

After moving to Amsterdam, Anne and Margot Frank were enrolled in school—Margot in public school and Anne in a Montessori school. Margot demonstrated ability in arithmetic, and Anne showed aptitude for reading and writing. Anne's friend, Hanneli Goslar, later recalled that from early childhood, Frank frequently wrote, although she shielded her work with her hands and refused to discuss the content of her writing.

In 1938, Otto Frank started a second company, Pectacon, which was a wholesaler of herbs, pickling salts, and mixed spices, used in the production of sausages. Hermann van Pels was employed by Pectacon as an advisor about spices. A Jewish butcher, he had fled Osnabrück with his family. In 1939, Edith Frank's mother came to live with the Franks, and remained with them until her death in January 1942.

In May 1940, Germany invaded the Netherlands, and the occupation government began to persecute Jews by the implementation of restrictive and discriminatory laws; mandatory registration and segregation soon followed. Otto Frank tried to arrange for the family to emigrate to the United States – the only destination that seemed to him to be viable – but this possibility was blocked from June 1941, as the U.S. government was concerned that people with close relatives still in Germany could be blackmailed into becoming Nazi spies. The Frank sisters were excelling in their studies and had many friends, but with the introduction of a decree that Jews could attend only Jewish schools, they were enrolled at the Jewish Lyceum. Anne became a friend of Jacqueline van Maarsen in the Lyceum. In April 1941, Otto took action to prevent Pectacon from being confiscated as a Jewish-owned business. He transferred his shares in Pectacon to Johannes Kleiman and resigned as director. The company was liquidated and all assets transferred to Gies and Company, headed by Jan Gies. In December, Otto followed a similar process to save Opekta. The businesses continued with little obvious change and their survival allowed Otto to earn a minimal income, but sufficient to provide for his family.

Time period chronicled in the diary
Before going into hiding

For her thirteenth birthday on 12 June 1942, Frank received a book she had shown her father in a shop window a few days earlier. Although it was an autograph book, bound with red-and-white checkered cloth and with a small lock on the front, Frank decided she would use it as a diary, and she began writing in it almost immediately. In her entry dated 20 June 1942, she lists many of the restrictions placed upon the lives of the Dutch Jewish population.

Otto and Edith Frank planned to go into hiding with the children on 16 July 1942, but when Margot received a call-up notice from the Zentralstelle für jüdische Auswanderung (Central Office for Jewish Emigration) on 5 July, ordering her to report for relocation to a work camp, they were forced to move the plan ten days forward. Shortly before going into hiding, Anne gave her friend and neighbour, Toosje Kupers, a book, a tea set, a tin of marbles, and the family cat for safekeeping. As the Associated Press reports: "'I'm worried about my marbles, because I'm scared they might fall into the wrong hands,' Kupers said Anne told her. 'Could you keep them for me for a little while?'"

Life in the Achterhuis

On the morning of Monday, 6 July 1942, the Frank family moved into their hiding place, a three-story space entered from a landing above the Opekta offices on the Prinsengracht, where some of his most trusted employees would be their helpers. This hiding place became known as the Achterhuis (translated as "Secret Annex" in English editions of the diary). Their apartment was left in a state of disarray to create the impression that they had left suddenly, and Otto left a note that hinted they were going to Switzerland. The need for secrecy forced them to leave behind Anne's cat, Moortje. As Jews were not allowed to use public transport, they walked several kilometres from their home. The door to the Achterhuis was later covered by a bookcase to ensure it remained undiscovered.

Victor Kugler, Johannes Kleiman, Miep Gies, and Bep Voskuijl were the only employees who knew of the people in hiding. Along with Gies' husband Jan Gies and Voskuijl's father Johannes Hendrik Voskuijl, they were the "helpers" for the duration of their confinement. The only connection between the outside world and the occupants of the house, they kept the occupants informed of war news and political developments. They catered to all of their needs, ensured their safety, and supplied them with food, a task that grew more difficult with the passage of time. Frank wrote of their dedication and of their efforts to boost morale within the household during the most dangerous of times. All were aware that, if caught, they could face the death penalty for sheltering Jews.

On 13 July 1942, the Franks were joined by the van Pels family: Hermann, Auguste, and 16-year-old Peter, and then in November by Fritz Pfeffer, a dentist and friend of the family. Frank wrote of her pleasure at having new people to talk to, but tensions quickly developed within the group forced to live in such confined conditions. After sharing her room with Pfeffer, she found him to be insufferable and resented his intrusion, and she clashed with Auguste van Pels, whom she regarded as foolish. She regarded Hermann van Pels and Fritz Pfeffer as selfish, particularly in regard to the amount of food they consumed. Sometime later, after first dismissing the shy and awkward Peter van Pels, she recognized a kinship with him and the two entered a romance. She received her first kiss from him, but her infatuation with him began to wane as she questioned whether her feelings for him were genuine, or resulted from their shared confinement. Anne Frank formed a close bond with each of the helpers, and Otto Frank later recalled that she had anticipated their daily visits with impatient enthusiasm. He observed that Anne's closest friendship was with Bep Voskuijl, "the young typist ... the two of them often stood whispering in the corner."

The young diarist

In her writing, Frank examined her relationships with the members of her family, and the strong differences in each of their personalities. She considered herself to be closest emotionally to her father, who later commented, "I got on better with Anne than with Margot, who was more attached to her mother. The reason for that may have been that Margot rarely showed her feelings and didn't need as much support because she didn't suffer from mood swings as much as Anne did." The Frank sisters formed a closer relationship than had existed before they went into hiding, although Anne sometimes expressed jealousy towards Margot, particularly when members of the household criticized Anne for lacking Margot's gentle and placid nature. As Anne began to mature, the sisters were able to confide in each other. In her entry of 12 January 1944, Frank wrote, "Margot's much nicer ... She's not nearly so catty these days and is becoming a real friend. She no longer thinks of me as a little baby who doesn't count."

Frank frequently wrote of her difficult relationship with her mother, and of her ambivalence towards her. On 7 November 1942 she described her "contempt" for her mother and her inability to "confront her with her carelessness, her sarcasm and her hard-heartedness," before concluding, "She's not a mother to me." Later, as she revised her diary, Frank felt ashamed of her harsh attitude, writing: "Anne, is it really you who mentioned hate, oh Anne, how could you?" She came to understand that their differences resulted from misunderstandings that were as much her fault as her mother's, and saw that she had added unnecessarily to her mother's suffering. With this realization, Frank began to treat her mother with a degree of tolerance and respect.

The Frank sisters each hoped to return to school as soon as they were able, and continued with their studies while in hiding. Margot took a shorthand course by correspondence in Bep Voskuijl's name and received high marks. Most of Anne's time was spent reading and studying, and she regularly wrote and edited her diary entries. In addition to providing a narrative of events as they occurred, she wrote about her feelings, beliefs, and ambitions, subjects she felt she could not discuss with anyone. As her confidence in her writing grew, and as she began to mature, she wrote of more abstract subjects such as her belief in God, and how she defined human nature.

Frank aspired to become a journalist, writing in her diary on Wednesday, 5 April 1944:

"I finally realized that I must do my schoolwork to keep from being ignorant, to get on in life, to become a journalist, because that's what I want! I know I can write ..., but it remains to be seen whether I really have talent ...

And if I don't have the talent to write books or newspaper articles, I can always write for myself. But I want to achieve more than that. I can't imagine living like Mother, Mrs. van Daan and all the women who go about their work and are then forgotten. I need to have something besides a husband and children to devote myself to! ...

I want to be useful or bring enjoyment to all people, even those I've never met. I want to go on living even after my death! And that's why I'm so grateful to God for having given me this gift, which I can use to develop myself and to express all that's inside me!

When I write I can shake off all my cares. My sorrow disappears, my spirits are revived! But, and that's a big question, will I ever be able to write something great, will I ever become a journalist or a writer?"

— Anne Frank

She continued writing regularly until her last entry of 1 August 1944.

Arrest

On the morning of 4 August 1944, the Achterhuis was stormed by a group of German uniformed police (Grüne Polizei) led by SS-Oberscharführer Karl Silberbauer of the Sicherheitsdienst. The Franks, van Pelses, and Pfeffer were taken to RSHA headquarters, where they were interrogated and held overnight. On 5 August they were transferred to the Huis van Bewaring (House of Detention), an overcrowded prison on the Weteringschans. Two days later they were transported to the Westerbork transit camp, through which by that time more than 100,000 Jews, mostly Dutch and German, had passed. Having been arrested in hiding, they were considered criminals and sent to the Punishment Barracks for hard labour.

Victor Kugler and Johannes Kleiman were arrested and jailed at the penal camp for enemies of the regime at Amersfoort. Kleiman was released after seven weeks, but Kugler was held in various work camps until the war's end. Miep Gies and Bep Voskuijl were questioned and threatened by the Security Police but not detained. They returned to the Achterhuis the following day, and found Anne's papers strewn on the floor. They collected them, as well as several family photograph albums, and Gies resolved to return them to Anne after the war. On 7 August 1944, Gies attempted to facilitate the release of the prisoners by confronting Silberbauer and offering him money to intervene, but he refused.

Although there have been persistent claims of betrayal by an informant, the source of the information that led the authorities to raid the Achterhuis has never been identified. Night watchman Martin Sleegers and an unidentified police officer investigated a burglary at the premises in April 1944 and came across the bookcase concealing the secret door. Tonny Ahlers, a member of the National Socialist Movement in the Netherlands (NSB), was suspected of being the informant by Carol Ann Lee, biographer of Otto Frank. Another suspect is stockroom manager Willem van Maaren. The Annex occupants did not trust him, as he seemed inquisitive regarding people entering the stockroom after hours. He once unexpectedly asked the employees whether there had previously been a Mr. Frank at the office. Lena Hartog was suspected of being the informant by Anne Frank's biographer Melissa

Müller. Several of these suspects knew one another and might have worked in collaboration. While virtually everyone connected with the betrayal was interrogated after the war, no one was definitively identified as being the informant.

In 2015, Flemish journalist Jeroen de Bruyn and Joop van Wijk, Bep Voskuijl's youngest son, wrote a biography, Bep Voskuijl, het zwijgen voorbij: een biografie van de jongste helper van het Achterhuis (Bep Voskuijl, the Silence is Over: A Biography of the Youngest Helper of the Secret Annex), in which they alleged that Bep's younger sister Nelly (1923–2001) could have betrayed the Frank family. According to the book, Bep's sister Diny and her fiancé Bertus Hulsman recollected Nelly telephoning the Gestapo on the morning of 4 August 1944. Nelly had been critical of Bep and their father, Johannes Voskuijl, helping the Jews. (Johannes was the one who constructed the bookcase covering the entrance to the hiding place.) Nelly was a Nazi collaborator between 1942 and 1946. Karl Silberbauer, the SS officer who received the phone call and made the arrest, was documented to say that the informer had "the voice of a young woman".

In 2016, the Anne Frank House published new research pointing to investigation over ration card fraud, rather than betrayal, as a plausible explanation for the raid that led to the arrest of the Franks. The report states that other activities in the building may have led authorities there, including activities of Frank's company. However, it does not rule out betrayal.

Deportation and death

On 3 September 1944, the group was deported on what would be the last transport from Westerbork to the Auschwitz concentration camp and arrived after a three-day journey. On the same train was Bloeme Evers-Emden, an Amsterdam native who had befriended Margot and Anne in the Jewish Lyceum in 1941. Bloeme saw Anne, Margot, and their mother regularly in Auschwitz, and was interviewed for her remembrances of the Frank women in Auschwitz in the television documentary The Last Seven Months of Anne Frank (1988) by Dutch filmmaker Willy Lindwer and the BBC documentary Anne Frank Remembered (1995).

Upon arrival at Auschwitz, the SS forcibly separated the men from the women and children, and Otto Frank was wrenched from his family. Those deemed able to work were admitted into the camp, and those deemed unfit for labour were immediately killed. Of the

1,019 passengers, 549—including all children younger than 15—were sent directly to the gas chambers. Anne Frank, who had turned 15 three months earlier, was one of the youngest people to be spared from her transport. She was soon made aware that most people were gassed upon arrival and never learned that the entire group from the Achterhuis had survived this selection. She reasoned that her father, in his mid-fifties and not particularly robust, had been killed immediately after they were separated.

With the other females not selected for immediate death, Frank was forced to strip naked to be disinfected, had her head shaved, and was tattooed with an identifying number on her arm. By day, the women were used as slave labour and Frank was forced to haul rocks and dig rolls of sod; by night, they were crammed into overcrowded barracks. Some witnesses later testified Frank became withdrawn and tearful when she saw children being led to the gas chambers; others reported that more often she displayed strength and courage. Her gregarious and confident nature allowed her to obtain extra bread rations for her mother, sister, and herself. Disease was rampant; before long, Frank's skin became badly infected by scabies. The Frank sisters were moved into an infirmary, which was in a state of constant darkness and infested with rats and mice. Edith Frank stopped eating, saving every morsel of food for her daughters and passing her rations to them through a hole she made at the bottom of the infirmary wall.

In October 1944, the Frank women were slated to join a transport to the Liebau labour camp in Upper Silesia. Bloeme Evers-Emden was slated to be on this transport, but Anne was prohibited from going because she had developed scabies, and her mother and sister opted to stay with her. Bloeme went on without them.

On 28 October, selections began for women to be relocated to Bergen-Belsen. More than 8,000 women, including Anne and Margot Frank, and Auguste van Pels, were transported. Edith Frank was left behind and later died from starvation. Tents were erected at Bergen-Belsen to accommodate the influx of prisoners, and as the population rose, the death toll due to disease increased rapidly. Frank was briefly reunited with two friends, Hanneli Goslar and Nanette Blitz, who were confined in another section of the camp. Goslar and Blitz survived the war, and later discussed the brief conversations they had conducted with Frank through a fence. Blitz described Anne as bald, emaciated, and shivering. Goslar noted Auguste van Pels was with Anne and Margot Frank, and was caring for Margot, who was severely ill. Neither of them saw Margot, as she was too weak to leave her bunk. Anne told Blitz and Goslar she believed her parents were dead, and for that reason she did not wish to live any longer. Goslar later estimated their meetings had taken place in late January or early February 1945.

In early 1945, a typhus epidemic spread through the camp, killing 17,000 prisoners. Other diseases, including typhoid fever, were rampant. Due to these chaotic conditions, it is not possible to say what ultimately caused Anne's death. Witnesses later testified Margot fell from her bunk in her weakened state and was killed by the shock. Anne died a few days after Margot. The exact dates of Margot and Anne's deaths were not recorded. It was long thought that their deaths occurred only a few weeks before British soldiers liberated the camp on 15 April 1945, but new research in 2015 indicated that they may have died as early as February of that year. Among other evidence, witnesses recalled that the Franks displayed typhus symptoms by 7 February, and Dutch health authorities reported that most untreated typhus victims died within 12 days of their first symptoms. After liberation, the camp was burned in an effort to prevent further spread of disease; the sisters were buried in a mass grave at an unknown location.

After the war, it was estimated that only 5,000 of the 107,000 Jews deported from the Netherlands between 1942 and 1944 survived. An estimated 30,000 Jews remained in the Netherlands, with many people aided by the Dutch underground. Approximately two-thirds of this group survived the war.

Otto Frank survived his internment in Auschwitz. After the war ended, he returned to

Amsterdam, where he was sheltered by Jan and Miep Gies as he attempted to locate his family. He learned of the death of his wife, Edith, in Auschwitz, but remained hopeful that his daughters had survived. After several weeks, he discovered Margot and Anne had also died. He attempted to determine the fates of his daughters' friends and learned many had been murdered. Sanne Ledermann, often mentioned in Anne's diary, had been gassed along with her parents; her sister, Barbara, a close friend of Margot's, had survived. Several of the Frank sisters' school friends had survived, as had the extended families of Otto and Edith Frank, as they had fled Germany during the mid-1930s, with individual family members settling in Switzerland, the United Kingdom, and the United States.

The Diary of a Young Girl

Publication

In July 1945, after the Red Cross confirmed the deaths of the Frank sisters, Miep Gies gave Otto Frank the diary and a bundle of loose notes that she had saved in the hope of returning them to Anne. Otto Frank later commented that he had not realized Anne had kept such an accurate and well-written record of their time in hiding. In his memoir, he described the painful process of reading the diary, recognizing the events described and recalling that he had already heard some of the more amusing episodes read aloud by his daughter. He saw for the first time the more private side of his daughter and those sections of the diary she had not discussed with anyone, noting, "For me it was a revelation ... I had no idea of the depth of her thoughts and feelings ... She had kept all these feelings to herself". Moved by her repeated wish to be an author, he began to consider having it published.

Frank's diary began as a private expression of her thoughts; she wrote several times that she would never allow anyone to read it. She candidly described her life, her family and companions, and their situation, while beginning to recognize her ambition to write fiction for publication. In March 1944, she heard a radio broadcast by Gerrit Bolkestein—a member of the Dutch government in exile, based in London—who said that when the war ended, he would create a public record of the Dutch people's oppression under German occupation. He mentioned the publication of letters and diaries, and Frank decided to submit her work when the time came. She began editing her writing, removing some sections and rewriting others, with a view to publication. Her original notebook was supplemented by additional notebooks and loose-leaf sheets of paper. She created pseudonyms for the members of the household and the helpers. The van Pels family became Hermann, Petronella, and Peter van Daan, and Fritz Pfeffer became Albert Düssell. In this edited version, she addressed each entry to "Kitty," a fictional character in Cissy van Marxveldt's Joop ter Heul novels that Anne enjoyed reading. Otto Frank used her original diary, known as "version A", and her edited version, known as "version B", to produce the first version for publication. He removed certain passages, most notably those in which Anne is critical of her parents (especially her mother), and sections that discussed Frank's growing sexuality. Although he restored the true identities of his own family, he retained all of the other pseudonyms.

Otto Frank gave the diary to the historian Annie Romein-Verschoor, who tried unsuccessfully to have it published. She then gave it to her husband Jan Romein, who wrote an article about it, titled "Kinderstem" ("A Child's Voice"), which was published in the newspaper Het Parool on 3 April 1946. He wrote that the diary "stammered out in a child's voice, embodies all the hideousness of fascism, more so than all the evidence at Nuremberg put together." His article attracted attention from publishers, and the diary was published in the Netherlands as Het Achterhuis (The Annex) in 1947, followed by five more printings by 1950.

It was first published in Germany and France in 1950, and after being rejected by several publishers, was first published in the United Kingdom in 1952. The first American edition, published in 1952 under the title Anne Frank: The Diary of a Young Girl, was positively reviewed. The book was successful in France, Germany, and the United States, but in the United Kingdom it failed to attract an audience and by 1953 was out of print. Its most noteworthy success was in Japan, where it received critical acclaim and sold more than 100,000 copies in its first edition. In Japan, Anne Frank quickly was identified as an important cultural figure who represented the destruction of youth during the war.

A play by Frances Goodrich and Albert Hackett based upon the diary premiered in New York City on 5 October 1955, and later won a Pulitzer Prize for Drama. It was followed by the 1959 movie The Diary of Anne Frank, which was a critical and commercial success. Biographer Melissa Müller later wrote that the dramatization had "contributed greatly to the romanticizing, sentimentalizing and universalizing of Anne's story." Over the years the popularity of the diary grew, and in many schools, particularly in the United States, it was included as part of the curriculum, introducing Anne Frank to new generations of readers.

In 1986 the Dutch Institute for War Documentation published the "Critical Edition" of the diary. It includes comparisons from all known versions, both edited and unedited. It includes discussion asserting the diary's authentication, as well as additional historical information relating to the family and the diary itself.

Cornelis Suijk—a former director of the Anne Frank Foundation and president of the U.S. Center for Holocaust Education Foundation—announced in 1999 that he was in the possession of five pages that had been removed by Otto Frank from the diary prior to publication; Suijk claimed that Otto Frank gave these pages to him shortly before his death in

1980. The missing diary entries contain critical remarks by Anne Frank about her parents' strained marriage and discuss Frank's lack of affection for her mother. Some controversy ensued when Suijk claimed publishing rights over the five pages; he intended to sell them to raise money for his foundation. The Netherlands Institute for War Documentation, the formal owner of the manuscript, demanded the pages be handed over. In 2000 the Dutch Ministry of Education, Culture and Science agreed to donate US$300,000 to Suijk's foundation, and the pages were returned in 2001. Since then, they have been included in new editions of the diary.

Reception

The diary has been praised for its literary merits. Commenting on Anne Frank's writing style, the dramatist Meyer Levin commended Frank for "sustaining the tension of a well-constructed novel", and was so impressed by the quality of her work that he collaborated with Otto Frank on a dramatization of the diary shortly after its publication. Levin became obsessed with Anne Frank, which he wrote about in his autobiography The Obsession. The poet John Berryman called the book a unique depiction, not merely of adolescence but of the "conversion of a child into a person as it is happening in a precise, confident, economical style stunning in its honesty".

In her introduction to the diary's first American edition, Eleanor Roosevelt described it as "one of the wisest and most moving commentaries on war and its impact on human beings that I have ever read." John F. Kennedy discussed Anne Frank in a 1961 speech, and said, "Of all the multitudes who throughout history have spoken for human dignity in times of great suffering and loss, no voice is more compelling than that of Anne Frank." In the same year, the Soviet writer Ilya Ehrenburg wrote of her: "One voice speaks for six million—the voice not of a sage or a poet but of an ordinary little girl."

As Anne Frank's stature, as both a writer and humanist has grown, she has been discussed specifically as a symbol of the Holocaust and more broadly as a representative of persecution. Hillary Clinton, in her acceptance speech for an Elie Wiesel Humanitarian Award in 1994, read from Anne Frank's diary and spoke of her "awakening us to the folly of indifference and the terrible toll it takes on our young," which Clinton related to contemporary events in Sarajevo, Somalia and Rwanda. After receiving a humanitarian award from the Anne Frank Foundation in 1994, Nelson Mandela addressed a crowd in Johannesburg, saying he had read Anne Frank's diary while in prison and "derived much encouragement from it." He likened her struggle against Nazism to his struggle against apartheid, drawing a parallel between the two philosophies: "Because these beliefs are patently false, and because they were, and will always be, challenged by the likes of Anne Frank, they are bound to fail." Also in 1994, Václav Havel said "Anne Frank's legacy is very much alive and it can address us fully" in relation to the political and social changes occurring at the time in former Eastern Bloc countries.

Primo Levi suggested Anne Frank is frequently identified as a single representative of the millions of people who suffered and died as she did because "One single Anne Frank moves us more than the countless others who suffered just as she did but whose faces have remained in the shadows. Perhaps it is better that way; if we were capable of taking in all the suffering of all those people, we would not be able to live." In her closing message in Müller's biography of Anne Frank, Miep Gies expressed a similar thought, though she attempted to dispel what she felt was a growing misconception that "Anne symbolises the six million victims of the Holocaust", writing: "Anne's life and death were her own individual fate, an individual fate that happened six million times over. Anne cannot, and should not, stand for the many individuals whom the Nazis robbed of their lives ... But her fate helps us grasp the immense loss the world suffered because of the Holocaust."

Otto Frank spent the remainder of his life as custodian of his daughter's legacy, saying, "It's a strange role. In the normal family relationship, it is the child of the famous parent who has the honour and the burden of continuing the task. In my case the role is reversed." He recalled his publisher's explaining why he thought the diary has been so widely read, with the comment, "He said that the diary encompasses so many areas of life that each reader can find something that moves him personally". Simon Wiesenthal expressed a similar sentiment when he said that the diary had raised more widespread awareness of the Holocaust than had been achieved during the Nuremberg Trials, because "people identified with this child. This was the impact of the Holocaust, this was a family like my family, like your family and so you could understand this."

In June 1999, Time magazine published a special edition titled "Time 100: The Most Important People of the Century". Anne Frank was selected as one of the "Heroes & Icons", and the writer, Roger Rosenblatt, described her legacy with the comment, "The passions the book ignites suggest that everyone owns Anne Frank, that she has risen above the Holocaust, Judaism, girlhood and even goodness and become a totemic figure of the modern world—the moral individual mind beset by the machinery of destruction, insisting on the right to live and question and hope for the future of human beings." He notes that while her courage and pragmatism are admired, her ability to analyze herself and the quality of her writing are the key components of her appeal. He writes, "The reason for her immortality was basically literary. She was an extraordinarily good writer, for any age, and the quality of her work seemed a direct result of a ruthlessly honest disposition."

Denials of authenticity and legal action

After the diary became widely known in the late 1950s, various allegations against the veracity of the diary and/or its contents appeared, with the earliest published criticisms occurring in Sweden and Norway.

In 1957, Fria ord ("Free Words"), the magazine of the Swedish neofascist organization National League of Sweden published an article by Danish author and critic Harald Nielsen, who had previously written anti-Semitic articles about the Danish-Jewish author Georg Brandes. Among other things, the article claimed that the diary had been written by Meyer Levin.

In 1958, at a performance of The Diary of Anne Frank in Vienna, Simon Wiesenthal was challenged by a group of protesters who asserted that Anne Frank had never existed, and who challenged Wiesenthal to prove her existence by finding the man who had arrested her. Wiesenthal indeed began searching for

Karl Silberbauer and found him in 1963. When interviewed, Silberbauer admitted his role, and identified Anne Frank from a photograph as one of the people arrested. Silberbauer provided a full account of events, even recalling emptying a briefcase full of papers onto the floor. His statement corroborated the version of events that had previously been presented by witnesses such as Otto Frank.

Opponents of the diary continued to express the view that it was not written by a teen, but was a hoax, with Otto Frank being accused of fraud.

In 1959, Otto Frank took legal action in Lübeck against Lothar Stielau, a school teacher and former Hitler Youth member who published a school paper that described the diary as "a forgery." The complaint was extended to include Heinrich Buddegerg, who wrote a letter in support of Stielau, which was published in a

Lübeck newspaper. The court examined the diary in 1960 and authenticated the handwriting as matching that in letters known to have been written by Anne Frank. They declared the diary to be genuine. Stielau recanted his earlier statement, and Otto Frank did not pursue the case any further.

In 1976, Otto Frank took action against Heinz Roth of Frankfurt, who published pamphlets stating that the diary was "a forgery." The judge ruled that if Roth was to publish any further statements he would be subjected to a fine of 500,000 German marks and a six-month jail sentence. Roth appealed against the court's decision. He died in 1978, and after a year his appeal was rejected.

Otto Frank mounted a lawsuit in 1976 against Ernst Römer, who distributed a pamphlet titled "The Diary of Anne Frank, Bestseller, A Lie". When a man named Edgar Geiss distributed the same pamphlet in the courtroom, he too was prosecuted. Römer was fined 1,500 Deutschmarks, and Geiss was sentenced to six months imprisonment. The sentence of Geiss was reduced on appeal, and the case was eventually dropped following a subsequent appeal because the statutory limitation for libel had expired.

With Otto Frank's death in 1980, the original diary, including letters and loose sheets, were willed to the Dutch Institute for War Documentation, which commissioned a forensic study of the diary through the Netherlands Ministry of Justice in 1986. They examined the handwriting against known examples and found that they matched. They determined that the paper, glue, and ink were readily available during the time the diary was said to have been written. They concluded that the diary is authentic, and their findings were published in what has become known as the "Critical Edition" of the diary. On 23 March 1990, the Hamburg Regional Court confirmed the diary's authenticity.

In 1991, Holocaust deniers Robert Faurisson and Siegfried Verbeke produced a booklet titled The Diary of Anne Frank: A Critical Approach, in which they revived the allegation that Otto Frank wrote the diary. Purported evidence, as before, included several contradictions in the diary, that the prose style and handwriting were not those of a teenager, and that hiding in the Achterhuis would have been impossible. In December 1993 the Anne Frank House in Amsterdam and the Anne Frank Fonds in Basel filed a civil lawsuit to prohibit further distribution of Faurisson and Verbeke's booklet in the Netherlands. On 9 December 1998 the Amsterdam District Court ruled in favour of the claimants, forbade any further denial of the authenticity of the diary and unsolicited distribution of publications to that effect, and imposed a penalty of 25,000 guilders per infringement.

Complaints regarding unabridged version

An unabridged edition of Anne Frank's work was published in 1995. This version included Anne's description of her exploration of her own genitalia and her puzzlement regarding sex and childbirth, a passage that had previously been edited out by Otto Frank. When Gail Horalek of Northville, Michigan, learned in March 2013 that her daughter's seventh-grade class was using this edition of the diary in class, she filed a complaint with the school district asking that an edited version be used instead. Horalek, who described the passage as pornographic, said the school should have obtained prior approval from parents before assigning the book. In 2010, school officials in Culpeper County, Virginia, stopped assigning the unabridged version after similar complaints were lodged.

Emer O'Toole of The Guardian noted that "we live in a society in which young women are taught to be ashamed of the changes that their bodies undergo at puberty – to be secretive about them, and even to pretend that they don't exist." Clem Bastow of Daily Life found the complaint "infuriating".

Legacy

On 3 May 1957, a group of citizens, including Otto Frank, established the Anne Frank Stichting in an effort to rescue the Prinsengracht building from demolition and to make it accessible to the public. The Anne

Frank House opened on 3 May 1960. It consists of the Opekta warehouse and offices and the Achterhuis, all unfurnished so that visitors can walk freely through the rooms. Some personal relics of the former occupants remain, such as movie star photographs glued by Anne to a wall, a section of wallpaper on which Otto Frank marked the height of his growing daughters, and a map on the wall where he recorded the advance of the Allied Forces, all now protected behind Perspex sheets. From the small room which was once home to Peter van Pels, a walkway connects the building to its neighbours, also purchased by the Foundation. These other buildings are used to house the diary, as well as rotating exhibits that chronicle aspects of the Holocaust and more contemporary examinations of racial intolerance around the world. One of Amsterdam's main tourist attractions, it received a record 965,000 visitors in 2005. The House provides information via the internet and offers exhibitions that in 2005 travelled to 32 countries in Europe, Asia, North America, and South America.

In 1963, Otto Frank and his second wife, Elfriede Geiringer-Markovits, set up the Anne Frank Fonds as a charitable foundation, based in Basel, Switzerland. The Fonds raises money to donate to causes "as it sees fit". Upon his death, Otto willed the diary's copyright to the Fonds, on the provision that the first 80,000 Swiss francs in income each year was to be distributed to his heirs. Any income above this figure is to be retained by the Fonds for use on whatever projects its administrators considered worthy. It provides funding for the medical treatment of the Righteous among the Nations on a yearly basis. The Fonds aims to educate young people against racism, and loaned some of Anne Frank's papers to the United States Holocaust Memorial Museum in Washington for an exhibition in 2003. Its annual report that year outlined its efforts to contribute on a global level, with support for projects in Germany, Israel, India, Switzerland, the United Kingdom, and the United States.

In 1997, the Anne Frank Educational Centre (Jugendbegegnungsstätte Anne Frank) was opened in the Dornbusch neighbourhood of Frankfurt, where Frank lived with her family until 1934. The Centre is "a place where both young people and adults can learn about the history of National Socialism and discuss its relevance to today."

The Merwedeplein apartment, where the Frank family lived from 1933 until 1942, remained privately owned until the 2000s. After becoming the focus of a television documentary, the building—in a serious state of disrepair—was purchased by a Dutch housing corporation. Aided by photographs taken by the Frank family and descriptions in letters written by Anne Frank, it was restored to its 1930s appearance. Teresien da Silva of the Anne Frank House and Frank's cousin, Bernhard "Buddy" Elias, contributed to the restoration project. It opened in 2005. Each year, a writer who is unable to write freely in his or her own country is selected for a year-long tenancy, during which they reside and write in the apartment. The first writer selected was the Algerian novelist and poet El-Mahdi Acherchour.

Anne Frank is included as one of the topics in the Canon of Dutch History, which was prepared by a committee headed by Frits van Oostrom and presented to the Minister of Education, Culture and Science, Maria van der Hoeven, in 2006; the Canon is a list of fifty topics that aims to provide a chronological summary of Dutch history to be taught in primary schools and the first two years of secondary school in the Netherlands. A revised version, which still includes her as one of the topics, was presented to the Dutch government on 3 October 2007.

In June 2007, "Buddy" Elias donated some 25,000 family documents to the Anne Frank House. Among the artefacts are Frank family photographs taken in Germany and the Netherlands and the letter Otto Frank sent his mother in 1945, informing her that his wife and daughters had perished in Nazi concentration camps.

In November 2007, the Anne Frank tree—by then infected with a fungal disease affecting the tree trunk—was scheduled to be cut down to prevent it from falling on the surrounding buildings. Dutch economist Arnold Heertje said about the tree: "This is not just any tree. The Anne Frank tree is bound up with the persecution of the Jews." The Tree Foundation, a group of tree conservationists, started a civil case to stop the felling of the horse chestnut, which received international media attention. A Dutch court ordered city officials and conservationists to explore alternatives and come to a solution. The parties built a steel construction that was expected to prolong the life of the tree up to 15 years. However, it was only three years later, on 23 August 2010, that gale-force winds blew down the tree. Eleven saplings from the tree were distributed to museums, schools, parks and Holocaust remembrance centres through a project led by the Anne Frank Center USA. The first sapling was planted in April 2013 at The Children's Museum of Indianapolis. Saplings were also sent to a school in Little Rock, Arkansas that was the scene of a desegregation battle, Liberty Park (Manhattan), which honours victims of the September 11 attacks, and other sites in the United States. Another horse chestnut tree honoring Frank was planted in 2010 at Kelly Ingram Park in Birmingham, Alabama.

Over the years, several films about Anne Frank appeared. Her life and writings have inspired a diverse group of artists and social commentators to make reference to her in literature, popular music, television, and other media. These include The Anne Frank Ballet by Adam Darius, first performed in 1959, and the choral work Annelies, first performed in 2005. The only known footage of the real Anne Frank comes from a 1941 silent film recorded for her newlywed next-door neighbour. She is seen leaning out of a second-floor window in an attempt to better view the bride and groom.

The couple, who survived the war, gave the film to the Anne Frank House.

In 1999, Time named Anne Frank among the heroes and icons of the 20th century on their list The Most Important People of the Century, stating: "With a diary kept in a secret attic, she braved the Nazis and lent a searing voice to the fight for human dignity". Philip Roth called her the "lost little daughter" of Franz Kafka. Madame Tussauds wax museum unveiled an exhibit featuring a likeness of Anne Frank in 2012. Asteroid 5535 Annefrank was named in her honour in 1995, after having been discovered in 1942.

43182790R00033

Made in the USA
Middletown, DE
20 April 2019